The Ghost Poetry Project

The Ghost Poetry Project

Nathan Curnow

PUNCHER & WATTMANN

First published in 2009 by Puncher and Wattmann
PO Box 441
Glebe NSW 2037

http://www.puncherandwattmann.com

puncherandwattmann@bigpond.com

National Library of Australia
Cataloguing-in-Publication entry:

Curnow, Nathan

The Ghost Poetry Project
ISBN   9781921450181

I. Title.

A821.3

Cover design by Matthew Holt

Printed by McPhersons Printing Group

This project has been assisted by the Australian Government through the Australia Council, its arts funding and advisory body.

Australian Government

Australia | **Council**
for the Arts

For Darcie, Scarlet, Rue

and

baby Alexis

Acknowledgements

Poems from this collection have been published in: *Island, Overland, Blast, Going Down Swinging, Flash: The International Short-Story Magazine, Blue Dog, Idiom 23, Four W, Page Seventeen, Harvest, Cutwater Anthology, Stylus, Foam:e, Famous Reporter, Blue Giraffe* and *qarrtsiluni.* Slater Bug/the Colour of Asphyxiation won the Bauhinia Poetry Prize.

For feedback, advice and support: Miles Allinson, Kevin Brophy, Kerryn Curnow, Ross Gillett, Francesca Haig, Peter Kirkpatrick, Paul Mitchell, Esther Ottaway, Ron Pretty, David Ryding, Ali Jane Smith and Alicia Sometimes

About the Author

As a child Nathan Curnow suffered 'night paralysis'. He could barely breathe due to an overwhelming sense of terror. A poet, playwright and performer, he has toured Australia and New Zealand and been featured widely on ABC radio.

Contents

Monte Cristo

Fremantle Arts Centre

Richmond Bridge

Elvira the Haunted Hearse

Bunyips Only Eat Avocadoes

why I am sleeping at ten haunted sites

The mechanical bunyip at Murray Bridge still rises
like the price of fear. Once I stood at the fence, fed him
a silver coin, set fire to his dirty water. And then he roared,
crashing the surface, breaking out of his inky trough. I ran
from the value of mum's twenty cents pleading barley
at the speed of fright.

Now for two dollars the motor of the beast begins
a new round of sleepless nights, the twisted trapdoor
of her mind releasing a monster that will not submerge.
Not for light or logic or my weight beside her, she suffers
each advance, until she overhears four magic words
bunyips only eat avocadoes.

*

he is the waiting dark
the Butcher the waiting dark
please Lord Jesus please Jesus Lord Jesus
I believe believe believe
                 wait
until your parents sleep
it is worse beneath the covers
I am the thought how the thought returns
don't breathe don't breathe
                 listen
he is closer now
if I reach him at least I know
there is too much space to fill with courage
fall back don't move

                        pray
they sleep
knives faster than prayer
sharp as light into your head
the Butcher the waiting the Butcher the dark

clock ticks the rhythm of the hit

                    *

and she is scared of ET, those blunt, protruding fingers,
the way spiders manage their legs on expedition, hesitant
yet deliberate he is reaching beneath the blankets, her body
a bouquet of unwelcome nerve endings, ET the botanist
at the end of the bed, ablaze with curiosity, closer, grips,
she cries out at last, the sound of her father's footsteps
as certain as his lack of belief, when he arrives words
fall like empty shells or a chocolate trail of M&M's
that will follow him out, she is alone again, recalling
the alien waddle, one by one, he is returning to her,
she can almost hear the crunching

                    *

Jesus is the picture is the picture in my pocket
is the picture in the pocket of my top
                              the Butcher
knows the picture knows pyjamas have a pocket
knows that Jesus will protect me in the dark
                    Jesus loves me
this I know   the Bible tells me so
the Bible says so many things

                                              the Butcher
            doesn't say a word

the Butcher the waiting the Butcher the dark
and the luminous hands of the clock
glowing like a ghost
                    Jesus rose from the dead
only after
he was slaughtered meat

                    *

Because the night is an eight-ball eye of a cow,
dark as the sludge inside your bones, fear locking
your delicate limbs deep beneath a tent of blankets.
I am returning as if I conquered the Butcher, as if
he lost his grip at last, descending with language,
my only defence, the one shot to defuse myself.

Because the nights are long, I will find new words
to pluck the eyeball out, testing them like avocadoes,
light or a picture card of Jesus. Let us reach together,
touch the monster's face, decipher the walls of the cave.
I will be calling your name. Call back to me.
There is always space for courage.

The Chifley Suite

On June 13, 1951, Ben Chifley, a long-time resident of the Kurrajong Hotel, skipped the Golden Jubilee Ball celebrations and retired to his room, number 214, in order to work. Later that evening he suffered a massive and fatal heart attack.

It is claimed a grey-suited man appears at the window pointing toward Parliament House. There are stories of physical contact, of cleaners being tapped on the shoulders and of people being tripped on the stairs.

Preparation

I make an appointment with the mystic in my tv guide, hire *The Shining* and watch it twice. I pay attention to Kubrick's use of colour and light, wonder if ghosts use similar tricks. I research Chifley, his policies, his life-long hatred of the banks. I read articles titled *Ghosts: All In The Mind* and *Tin Foil Hats Really Work*.

My wife buys three stones for their spiritual powers, says they need to be touching my skin. She wants me to practice holding them as if it's easy to get that wrong. And all the sachets in the hotel room I am meant to swipe for her collection. She just loves the trim of their packaging. It's not stealing if they expect to replace them.

I am also in the market for a handycam to capture the shadow on disc, to record my face when I choose to run, to establish which stone I threw first. I have lost them already, forgotten their names along with their particular charms and I consider it a sign of the ghost I'm expecting when my mystic does not turn up.

Canberra

From the air it is an outbreak of housing estates
surrounded by paddocks with pock scars of dams.
The only bodies of water close to full were approved
by bureaucrats. The fountain works around the clock
except when it breaks down. You know it's broken
when you don't see it working. But that's the only time.
The flag-pole is a national tuning fork or a frame
for a giant tin-hat, if our politicians have one good idea
it will block the radio-waves. High-tech security,
like the streets designed to keep spies from getting out.
Everything is disguised to look like an office—the cafes,
churches and playgrounds. Or a photocopier inside
an office, a new model with ramps and screen panels
that is waiting to show you how it doesn't work.
Just the sight of it pisses you off.

Stealing a Bird from a Serpent

-Mr Hallorann, what is in room 237?
-Nothin. There ain't nothin in room 237.

—The Shining

the room number dangling from the key in the lock,
drool hanging from Danny's lips, Mr Hallorann shining
to the pitch of needles, the smooth pan around the room
up the stairs beyond the bed and toward the door ajar
a slow hand reaching, pushing open, the theatre of the bath
in the distance, a shower curtain drawn as white as the ghost
behind it, extending her arm, pulling back the veil, the lure
of her impassive face, presenting her body like a tomb
of herself, lifts one foot above the edge, in perfect line
her perfect breasts, the hair between her legs, she points
a toe toward the floor, steps forward as if she floats,
limbs that hang as long as the dead, drapes her arms
around his neck, taking her waist he presses in
as if stealing a bird from a serpent, her sour lesions
reflected in the mirror, the putrid decay of the bath
drowning forever as he caresses her sores, she laughs
as he stumbles back, reaching for him the way
he reached her, tasting the rotting flesh

Rosa

Her trolley stacked as high as herself, loaded
with sprays and bottles, Rosa pushes her supplies
to the door of each room, worlds in single issue.
She abandons her cargo, draws light on the damage,
her products undefeated, the brittle bulb of her dog
in the corridor at the end of the vacuum cord.
Like a martial art, the crisp stroke of her hand
returns the bed to its seams. She chops the pillows,
wields sachets, soaps and complimentary pens.
Every world remade by one o'clock, the law
is the same for each, except for that room
at the top of the stairs, seems none of the guests
have noticed. How the tiny shampoo turns itself
every year on the day of his death, she enters
three times, with each click of the door—
ninety degrees to the left.

Prior Knowledge

a scream
> as I strike the shower taps

a scream
> as I pull the curtain
>> entrapping myself

warm vapour rising
> friend of the apparition

washing faster than usual I can't help but peek out
expecting an angry god
> the unseen room

> I have checked the wardrobes

I will have to check again
> when the books I stacked
> fall onto the floor
> I hear the sound of a collapsing man
>> or the sound
>> of prior knowledge

I step out of the shower
> shining

In No Half-Blooded Way

I saw death... a banker... he opened his mouth
and it suddenly became this huge mouth like a whale

—Robert Hughes

no words
no crack of the jaw
death undoes his mouth like a suit,
stretches an open throat, sharpens a ramp
at the edge of his teeth into the well-funded dark

collapsing
from your bed onto the floor
you battled in no half-blooded way
bargained a rate of return, an amount to invest
how the trace of your savings might appear

at the window
now the trees have grown
blocking whatever you are pointing out
an escape plan perhaps, lost in opposition
wanting control of the house again

The Footage

The footage confirms it is just a room, a fly lands
for a third time on the bench, rubbing its legs, an evil genius
igniting oomph from the wires of itself.

Despite a thousand eyes the body is proven best
by a quick massage, tweaking the equipment, slicking
the prongs, captain of the quick turn-around.

Resuming its flight-path, a holding pattern
tracing a geometrical ghost. Even in fast-forward
it is just a room, a fly spinning shapes out of nothing.

The Spoils

soap, conditioner, moisturiser
coffee, sugar and cookies
tea bags, mints, a small notepad
along with a hotel pen

something is missing
her Kurrajong collection
one item short of complete
the tiny bottle I refused to touch

why did you leave the shampoo behind?

Old Adelaide Gaol

Built in 1840, Old Adelaide Gaol is a macabre structure of cells, gargoyles and high stone walls. By the time of its closure in 1988 it had held three hundred thousand prisoners.

Forty-five people, including one woman, were hanged at the gaol. Executions were conducted outside the front gates before being moved inside to a portable gallows. Hangings also took place in the A Wing of the New Building and in the Hanging Tower when it was finally completed. The last execution was carried out in 1964.

Paranormal events such as noises, figures, orbs of light and unexplainable physical contact have all been said to occur inside the gaol walls. However it is the New Building, built in 1879, which is responsible for many encounters. A smiling ghost dressed in black with a moustache and long side-burns has often been reported at the top left hand side of the staircase.

Gaol Cat

Clink, the gaol cat, amplifying silence, saunters
past my open cell. On a self-guided tour she triggers
sensor lights, plays the keys of an invisible keyboard.

The fluoro shudders its arctic light, snaps brittle
the mannequin's gaze. Ignoring cheap exhibits
of history she wanders out toward the gargoyles.

Stuck beneath turrets their twisted faces protest
the unseen punch, torn by the throat into the after-life,
the head is the crown of a knot, the body a tail

that twitches at first hanging for an hour from eight.
She rolls on the trap, exposing her belly, juggles
a sky of falling fish. Or she sinks her claws

into the burial ground, the necklace of the gaol,
scratches up against the whipping frame.
Please do not play with the ropes or irons.

Wandering back, a high-priestess of a temple
made of stone. Barely dusk, and now the ghosts,
castellations of courage crumbling.

Ghost Tour Guide

The tour begins, just two of us as the pink woolwash sky
drains away. The scream of the flight-path, bleak shadows
burst over the razor-wire snap of walls.

He says he has a way with ghosts, a way of pissing them off.
He begins the night defining his terms, warning the poet
of language—the word ghost is like God

you'll be asked to prove it, everything loaded with
interpretation. See, I believe in ghosts but I don't say that.
There are two different types of hauntings.

The first is residual, a past event, stuck on repetitive loop.
Call it imprint or playback. I call it, residual, a buzz word
at the moment. Intelligent, is when a Spirit responds

directly to your presence. Which seems to happen to me.
I take too many photos, I have a way of pissing them off.
(Residual, a past event, stuck on repetitive loop.)

Most sightings in here occur after twelve, you're all mine until
then. You know I've begun writing a book as well.
(My sentence being written.)

Some Final Regard

Elizabeth Woolcock was executed in 1873 for poisoning her abusive husband.
She had attempted to hang herself years before but failed when the beam
broke.

                                    the noose is a turnkey
the trap is a box I will not have to kick myself
the rope is good rope, the beam will not break
I have tired of the weight of dry earth, and stone
never turned to bread for me, I had to turn to men
now they come at even pace, it is better to expect it
let them pinion my arms tight like wings, say prayers
I could not have imagined, everything measured
down to the drop, no need to keep the secret of this
I will hold the asters your wife picked me, walk past
my open grave, the spade that will hurl a heap of lime
onto my fresh cut corpse, let the doctor inspect it
death from violence, this time I will not return
free from gossip, some final regard
a hood to hide the bruising

Ghost Tour (New Building)

man in black with a smiling face
in the dark behind the gate, we are sitting
on his stairway, he is peering down
from behind the gantry cage, cell doors
burst out in strict order, sheet lightning
of the flash, my guide on a trigger
like paparazzi, switched to automatic

the sound returns, ringing out
like the echo of a ballroom, a pounding
cane on the walkway above, a rack
of billiard balls breaking open, dropping
deep into the building's well, all sides
surrounded by stone, buried alive
the heart of this tomb beating

Poe

Poe

Poe

At three am

my cell is a cold oven painted cream
the brow of the doorway set heavy rivets
are perfect welts the bulk of a submarine
slamming the peep hole releases a dark face
framed the globe in my bedside lamp blows
the door wide open my subsequent breath
as a figure waits permission stalled before
the signal bell sentenced to my room cursing
in the corner it bemoans the dark the cell door
slams shut on us both the sound of a wrist gnawed
wet for escape desperate to release the vein

Jawless Trap

...and sometimes you close your eyes
and see the place where you used to live...
—*The Killers*

fear is a mirrored face reflecting
the face of a mirror yourself repeating
a puzzle of the present confronting/ignoring
how tightly the illusion fits

and in the distance the house returning
the boy in his brother's pyjamas
the end of a hallway door swings open
she is washing his corpse again

this jawless trap this ricochet passage
always a corner approaching
domino-chained a certain throbbing
convinced you have already fallen

if you loved him keep his casket clean
sink your hand in the rat-mother's nest
a mound of padding pink with litter
she gathers them still giving birth

clutching the frame like excavation
you bury the strange/familiar face
forgetting you know how to forget
the last place you think fear is

My Guide Returns

My guide returns to my cell at six am. We talk about the night. I confirm the check-out time before he leads me to breakfast. I ordered coffee, croissants, fresh-fruit. I bow my head but he keeps grace brief, then excuses himself for a moment. I love coffee in the morning and there is time to enjoy it, there really is nothing to pack.

I have a hunch my guide is saying prayers outside, so I call him back in for a blessing. I ask him some questions, give him a letter I wrote, along with a kiss on the cheek. They bind my arms, lead me onto the trap. I imagine the jerk of the rope. My eyes are shut tight because I want this over. Let me drop into the noose of sleep.

Picton

Picton, one hour from Sydney, is said to be Australia's most haunted town. With a fascinating colonial history that includes much tragedy it boasts over twenty haunted buildings, along with haunted cemeteries, bridges and the foreboding Picton Tunnel.

In 1916 Emily Bollard was walking through the tunnel to visit her brother on the other side. Struck by the train from Thirlmere her body was carried all the way out to the road, although some claim she had to be collected piece by piece.

My accommodation was Room 11 at the George IV Inn, built in 1839 beside the Stonequarry Creek. A glowing crucifix is said to appear on the wall beside the bed, and strange 'dragging' noises have been heard outside. Upon checking in I was told of the recent stay of a railway worker who had been woken by something tapping him in the middle of the forehead.

Room 11

surrounded by wreaths in deathly green
    wallpaper wilts at the seams
                from my open doorway
    the beer garden sings
plates and glasses clink like leg irons
    the owner confesses
             he avoids his own cellar
because convicts were chained to the walls
    he turns off lights
             that he knows he turned off
    but refuses to say it's haunted
            business both ways
ghost-hunters check in
    corporates park weekend bikes
    their bitches on phones disguised in leather
            spokes burn as hot as my ribs
    wallpaper wilts
I am as weathered as a teddy left upon a child's grave
    contemplating the tunnel
            its reported cold spots
            let me bathe in the bath of a ghost

St Mark's Cemetery (Ghost Tour)

Ley-lines ignite between Heaven and Earth, lightning
of the change. Clouds pack into a plot of sky stained
dark as moss-patched lids. Kittens in long grass, tourists
roam the grounds pouncing among a showroom of beds,
peering beneath tablets pried open by time and the dumb
brute strength of trees. We bend toward each gaping trap
sniffing each hole for remains, bright eyes of torches
reaching empty cans and the sick cloth of plastic bags.

No sign of the dog buried in the yard, a black phantom
that chases tails. We return to our patient tour guide—
our defender from irate priests. Gathered to the curb,
evading local hoons, we prowl around empty buildings.
Photos of dust are grey balls of wool, everyone whet
with interest. At the Old Railway Hotel somebody cries—
there is a figure at the window. We spring for cameras.
Our tour guide says—*that's because people live there.*

Burning Snakes and Donuts

We are worked by car horns and whistling hoons
that circle on Friday nights. They lean from windows
without spilling a drop, baring sharp sticks of teeth.
Roaring at us, words urgent and witless, garbled
as EVP. Obscured by the din of the latest speakers,
their cars stink of Cougars and weed. Packed
with menace and nowhere to go they taste the thrill
of declaration, the shriek of rubber, burning snakes
and donuts, fanatics of traces on bitumen. And us
as we assert ourselves in the corners of the town,
electrified by simple shapes and the chance of
meeting death. As if challenging life, the straps
and buckles that have held us until now, safe
enough to push toward the wild of the unknown.
I confront the darkness with the venom of being,
tonight none of these streets are safe, geared to
believing I can stare death down with company
and a torch.

Picton Tunnel

sharp as a hairpin
the open mouth swallows
a frenzy of torch lights
as if fishing for tonsils
each brick infected
with the graffiti of vandals
a ceiling char-grilled
from burnt-out cars
approaching the corners
of built-in safety holes
spaces on display
our waiting coffins
the thrill of assembly
squeals and apologies
that distant eddy tips
the jugs of our eyes
thrashed by the wind
of a thousand bus stops
we work harder than story
for a glimpse of a ghost
or a groan that sounds like
each of us embittered
when some loser clicks
his torch back on

turn it off turn it off turn it off

This Knot

Waiting like a child with tangled hair, to be straightened
from the scalp, my spirit worked from flesh and bone, this knot
a lifetime's achievement. Staring down the tunnel I recall
how it felt the year I had nothing published. As bleak as graffiti
sprayed at the entrance—*Satan Fucks These Walls*. I wonder
if I have peaked already, overdrawn on my B for English.
Darkness skittles my skull full of words. I am a ghost
that approaches, then trips. Or a vandal in a vault shaking
the casket to hear the rattle of what remains. This knot,
as colourful pin-pricks of light burst at the tunnel mouth.
Sceptical of these tired eyes, what they make of
dust and distance, I gaze toward these tiny flames—
I write suspicious of the craft. Remaining open
to whatever comes although it becomes entangled.
I see flashes of light. My tingling scalp. Something
keeps tugging me back.

Ghost Train

the lights divide us, literally
we are bodies in the dirt, at the walls
a young girl cowering in a ball at my feet
we hit our torches, we trust our screams
turning to each other for confirmation it feels
so stupid to ask, because we all know we saw it
we just can't believe, a ghost train, I mean,
as if, four glowing lights speeding toward us
disappearing over our heads, when we threw
ourselves across limbs, torsos, our throats
delivered hearts to mouths, swallowing
the rocks and with the same single mind
that declared *everyone for themselves*
we switch off our torches one more time—
sounds like a conductor punching tickets

Playing Chicken With Trucks

*Outside Picton is a stretch of road once patrolled by the axe-murderer, John
Lynch. Local teenagers have also been known to go there and play chicken
with trucks, which may or may not explain the amount of 'road ghost'
sightings.*

you want to stay on your feet
        cause you're fucked if you trip
        you get hit and I'm pissing off
this here's the best spot for first-time starting
            yeah road's as long as my dick
barely five metres to the other side
shortest run of your life
          and don't look down the headlights
          you'll want to but
they're a gate and you won't come back
don't wait for me either
        I go by sound
        shut my eyes for a better buzz
           imagine how you look
to that bloke in the cabin
you're a road-ghost then you're gone
          better than a hit of amphetamines
            he won't ever fall asleep
          replaying what he saw
          between bug-squash and rain
and you'll be deaf for the next ten minutes
but the scream of exhaust brakes means you're still alive
          get over there check out that ditch
            you ready it's coming
like a ferry on fire
          hey looks like you're passing another Fox

Monte Cristo

Monte Cristo Homestead in the town of Junee is reported to be Australia's most haunted house. Built by Christopher William Crawley between 1876 to 1885, the classic Victorian mansion was part of a tightly-run estate up until his death in 1910. His wife Elizabeth Crawley, dressed like Queen Victoria, spent the next twenty-three years as a recluse, leaving Monte Cristo on only two occasions.

Monte Cristo's history of gruesome events includes: the death of an infant pushed down a stairwell; a sick boy burned alive when his boss set fire to his bed; a maid that committed suicide by throwing herself from the balcony; Harold Steel, who was chained to the Dairy wall by his mother for forty years; and also in the Dairy, the caretaker, Jack Simpson, who was murdered by a local teenager in 1961.

Reg and Olive Ryan bought Monte Cristo in 1963 and have restored it to full Victorian glory. It is lavishly furnished for its ten resident ghosts and is visited regularly by psychics, mediums and tv shows. The Ryan family have also experienced many disturbing events, like the morning they found their kitten mutilated on the kitchen floor.

Monte Cristo is open to tourists and ghost-hunters, and hosts Australia's longest running private ball.

Sails and Anvils

Upon arrival I will be the working poet cocked
for inspiration, directing my hosts with a pen's arrow
from the signs of my splitting headache. Inside
the plane the cabin of my head is rocked by
turbulence. Great sails and anvils are bright
arctic pages, the story of a doomed expedition.
This is the lesson—do not stay with poets
the night before flying out, drinking ensues
and they just want to have sex or complain
about their rejections. I left them moaning,
friends of mine, making love like friends,
bearing all but their vocabularies, competing
in wild noises. Aren't we all falling, our egos
packed with a plastic whistle to draw attention?
If the plane lands safely there is a rental car
waiting, some compartment I can crash in.
Another brittle booth, certain to betray me
when the impact finally comes. I am cranky
this morning, hurtling toward the chapter of
my decline. But with a pen and a pose I go
to work as if spirited by questions of 'soul'.
I just want to get off. Go, get fucked.
We are turning into cloud.

Float for Good

Reg monitors his heart at the kitchen table, cuffed to his BP machine. He says ghost-hunters spread powder on black plastic to trap the footprints of apparitions. It was almost something supernatural, the way he felt drawn to the house. As if he is meant to be here to fulfil some role. Olive serves up tea and biscuits.

She takes comfort in the noise of the television that mutters around the clock. It drowns out the ghosts that call her name. Olive doesn't want to believe. She knows the kind of people that delve too deep, some guests prowl the grounds until dawn. She has learnt to live here. Her coping strategies are secrets of how to remain.

Reg fears retirement more than ghosts. He rebuilt the ballroom himself. When we dance around the subject of the after-life he says he tries to do his best. There is always someone to screw you over, but it is better to be kind. He leans across the table with a glint in his eye, says, there are enough *hard* people in this world.

It's the clues that are buried in their conversation. Olive asks what room I chose. She wants to know what kind of night to expect based on the history of the house. At the point of farewell they will wave me off and call out, *bye for now*. As if they are sure I'll return or just want to remind me that endings are not so simple.

Reg monitors his heart at the kitchen table, proving his electrical field. His current flows through the walls and out to the stables, across the dance-floor at the charity ball. Olive wears her tiara one night a year, people come from all over the world. And no one bothers to mention the ghosts, all eager to float for good.

Bandit

The dog attempts to fill the garden with fury
then flashes his oily belly. On his back in the dirt
he licks the air on automatic, thanking the universe.

From the garden he drags a desiccated rabbit,
a dog-chew twice his size, a macabre greeting card
delivered to my feet, an omen as night approaches.

The carcass is stuck in a bounding stride, a grim
portrayal of the ground to cover. Death is a package
worth tearing to strips, just a mouthful of sticky fur.

Burying himself in a mask of ribs, in the cavities
of a curse, he growls an invitation to rage like this,
a battle-cry despite the odds. The way Blackie

the cat, years before, sensing something drawing near
chose to leap from the balcony, backing herself,
escaped never to be seen again.

In The Telling

Reg hands me the phone before the ghost tour begins and I suddenly become a Priest, a confidant of last week's guest, the fear still in his voice. I am given advice on how to survive. The kid tells me not to play my iPod. He says his sound was interfered with so he threw it across the room. (I had downloaded Wolfmother for courage.)

Walking through the stables where a boy burnt to death, he says his camera caught on fire. *Coincidence?* he asks, asking himself, wanting answers from someone else. Over his mum's dead body he plans to get a tattoo to remember the mansion by. He saw a girl at midnight waiting in the garden, inviting him over to play.

But perhaps the phone call is just a pre-emptive strike, like each one of Reg's yarns. We are shown reports from old tv shows to help put us in the mood. By this we know what behaviours to manifest, how to structure a tale of our own. If we become overwhelmed we can retreat back to Olive in the rocker watching television.

Candles are lit. Reg is dressed in black. I turn on my handycam. But I am thinking of Olive and the people she's sat with, the conversation upon their return. Or whether they recline together in pale wash, Olive too tired to hear confession. A camera bursting into flames can sound so familiar without some creativity in the telling.

The Handycam Works

the equipment is good
> the handycam works
but my sidekick seizes up in the house
> squares and pixels snap-freeze on the screen
> we are a colourful tray of cubes
> a kaleidoscope of trauma
the camera reverts to Basic Sketching 101
> it fills its grid with simple lines
> structure/size/proportion

> closer to the Boys' room
where the walls drip with blood
> date and time in the corner alluding
> to temporal disorientation
past and present mince together
> bewildered digits reach
new time is spun as figures impose
> bumping into figures

the Boys' room behind us
> normal function resumes
> we are restored to our familiar forms
my German-made lens disciplines itself
> shutting out grief with work
stepping back into the hallway
> shooting down the dark
a pale shape is revealed on the stairs
> lit by the battery-power it's drained
> and the footage it has erased

Monte Cristo

hackles rising
how the body burns
the frothing mouths of pets
baby in night clothes in a hot, hot room
always an infant falling
face at the window, purple-faced
master of the pregnant maids
daughters beneath green-lined umbrellas
the sudden lurching Phaeton
chained to the wall, pining for mother
a grip that wrings the neck
a collar box that remains forbidden
a hand that wants to reach
lustre vases with dumbbell drops
the four-tiered walnut whatnot
the Ronisch piano playing itself
humming birds neatly pressed
smoke from the chimney
looping back into the chimney
an old lady dressed in black
priest with a silver crucifix
suicide stains the steps
portraits in birds eye maple frames
large oval mirror reflecting
the gold-plated clock chiming the hour
always an infant falling

I am the village of Loftus proclaimed
I am the Mount of Christ
I am your inexplicable tears
I am attaching myself to your chest

Bunyips (2)

The Butcher, the waiting, the Butcher, the dark,
I intended to be braver than this, to write a mansion
of words, chain myself to the night, howl down
what ever brushed past. I am still the boy too sick
to move though my bed is set alight, lungs crushed
by familiar terror and the rat poison of tobacco.

All the things I ever burnt, the remains of the house
I grew up in, the sound of the child who dared cry out,
the graves I imagined were mine, crammed tonight
into a four-poster bed smothering this big idea.
I should open the door, step into the hallway,
investigate the noise.

But the night is an eight-ball eye of a cow.
Portraits turn on feeble minds. They will rear me
back into dust-covered chairs, the moonlit chill of
antiques. I had hoped to trade, to deal in words.
Some poetic freedom-fighter. The sound of a kitten
mutilated, stomach emptied onto the floor.

Fremantle Arts Centre

A fine example of Colonial Gothic architecture, Fremantle Arts Centre was originally a Lunatic Asylum built by convicts out of local limestone in the 1860s.

Subject to a monotonous daily routine, 'lunatics' would be woken by a gong at sunrise and herded out into the courtyard, a shed being their only shelter from the elements. At night the Asylum was filled by the screams of the disturbed. Inmates were strapped to their beds, locked in straight jackets, mittens or imprisoned in dark isolation cells.

Based on regular reports of paranormal activity, some regard the old Lunatic Asylum as the most haunted building in Western Australia. Three resident ghosts are said to be responsible for cold spots, footsteps, and the whistling that is heard in the corridors.

I spent the night in the Painting Studio, the room of an Irish woman who committed suicide by throwing herself from the first-floor window. Driven to madness by the abduction of her child she is said to walk the corridors with a hurricane lamp still looking for her daughter.

Lice

My wife might be a happy chimp
picking through my hair, checking for lice
before I leave, displaying loyalty and affection.
Our daughters are polluting us, eggs stuck
to the mesh of their heads. We tried spraying
them with eucalyptus, tying hair back in buns.
Grouchy farms, they go to sleep harvesting
pre-historic beasts. Nymphs crawl edges of
delicate dreams sucking blood from itchy scalps.
But none of our girls will let us cut their hair.
We break our backs on the shoulder of the bath
combing soapy gunk through wild jungles
full of villainous life. Trapping the creatures
against the walls of our thumbs, pressing
to hear them burst. Each *click* is the sound
of good parenting, a tick in a Goodall report.
My wife shaves my head, a crude solution,
one acceptable for mature males. I grunt at her,
clearly unimpressed with her use of simple tools.

*

Upon induction to the Lunatic Asylum the hair of both male and female 'prisoners' was completely removed. Overcrowding was a constant issue, inmates receiving one bath a week with water shared by up to three people.

I imagine the person cutting the hair knew that most would never be released. Incarcerated for their own protection they would remain there until they died. So the shears might have seemed an act of kindness, each stroke a deep and pleasing good. Or else the cutter heard the curse of every snip—there will be no lice in death.

Slater Bug   Colour of Asphyxiation

Slater bug locks its soft brush of legs
behind the armoured curl. A grey-plated pea
sits cushioned in her hand, palm-lines
make a careful cup. She opens it wider,
I want to keep him, she says, the little ball
drops to the floor. We transfer him into
a washed-out tub that smells of leftovers.

                    Tonight I am an inmate, a scab, a crust
                    that sets on a drop of paint. Studio fumes
                    smear my head, dab me the colour of
                    asphyxiation. I am a shape unintended
                    beyond the window pane with a headache
                    no doctor can fix. I must encourage myself
                    into occupation, a cure of mental disease.

She sprinkles him with blades of grass,
we fix a plastic sky, punch diamond holes
into his terrible drum, granting asylum
from the garden. Trapped, he remains
neatly sealed. Shaking him will not help.
But he has got to understand for the good
of himself, how much love she has to give.

                    A forest of easels are locked in with me
                    leaning back on single clogs. They skate
                    in reverse toward the corner of the room,
                    leaving me exposed. Locks and bolts
                    become agitated, which means nurse
                    will stroke my shell, turn me, prod me,
                    kiss my cheek, throw me rations as reward.

I discover the bucket beneath her teddies.
The sky is torn but there was no escape.
His plates have set before I could teach her
the importance of release. He is a gloomy pod,
a dismal package of all our best intentions.
As if he knew there was no point feeling
anything beyond his reach.

        Surely this is delirium. I am not a bug
        the world forgot. My fingers are typing out
        isolation, spidering across these padded walls.
        Not fouling myself, not shredding my clothes
        or the stuffing of horsehair and coir.
        Dawn is always the resounding gong.
        Not howling. I am not quiet.

Unequivocal Light

my goose bumps standing over me
silence alerts me to the noise of silence

the pulse in my ears or bare feet on boards
I am staring through the door's glass panels

to the EXIT lamp at the end of the corridor
where the ghost-story becomes the ghost

distinguishing them is as pointless as calling
the Devil from the Angel of Death

at four am the street sweeper brushes
the room with unequivocal light

a swift exhibition like a beating of wings
the knuckled man inside me clenching

this remarkable darkness in secret places
the gutters of my aching flesh

stiff with the drawing heaving up
leaking from the purse of my mouth

Open Window

she imagines the wind will paint her face
in a moment of no great concern
actions will be swift and without herself
a performance she will not interrupt

nothing will snag her at the open window
let the sky deal the weight of grief
she will end the cries reaching into
her dreams determined to pull her out

as quickly as it takes to steal a child
she will release without a sound
though she is cast as true as a lead sinker
tears straight as a strip of bedding

approaching the blessed drum of stone
falling sideways with sideways eyes
the sound of a common stitch—picked
a posy of faces looking down

each movement comes bearing
its own sorrowful witness
she braces herself against surprise
filling the pillow of her chest with air

suddenly the steps

Love Note On Serviette

Inspired by an account of the 'prisoner' who in 1899 threw a love poem weighted by a stone over the wall of the Asylum.

my own fond love
this portion find your path
I feel myself beyond myself
am able to choose this rock
to traffic these words
put your cold on me
gazing forever upward
throw me something
I love you I love you
lavender is making sense

notice the rocks
I have practiced this
promise me yourself
I found a secret passage
beneath the Peppercorn trees
it is forbidden by the Pope
instead he blessed me
with a hole in the wall
I have imagined
that you wave

much like you throw
throw me something
be my gracious garden
your voice climbs over
a lavender ladder
do you want to
hear me breathing
I am feeling myself
the stiff sin of a sinner
the Pope is always watching

The Floor is a Collection

I place the manuscript in order
across the width of the hallway
to see if the ghost concurs.
Perhaps by morning she will
prove herself a critic, exposing
the error of sequence.

I retreat around the corner,
abandoning papers, supposing
them neatly rearranged—
thoughtful encouragement,
a gentle invitation to
re-consider my emphasis.

Or else there might be noises—
tearing, chewing, then
a kind of regurgitation,
what a teacher hears
seconds before the white
paste of a spitball is fired.

The floor is a collection
of occasional creaks but that
might be the imagination.
The ghost seems to approve
or she does not exist or
is simply illiterate.

Anxiety

My psychologist believes I am only possessed
by issues of unresolved anger. She thinks writing
will help me make the most of myself, isolating
the disturbance. I keep forgetting the world
is a nice place to live, that it wants to love me
and be loved in return. Panic attacks come
as busloads of Sumo, crushing me flat
between folds of skin.

Today I am stuck with adhesive electrodes
that monitor palpitations. Next is a lung test
that will attempt to explain why I work so hard
to breathe. I suspect my GP is trying to prove
that I have an overactive imagination. Perhaps
I also belong to that four per-cent most likely
to report apparitions. Fantasy-prone,

what I seem to be experiencing are hiccups
in the cycle. Suggestion haunts the dark rooms
of my body until I feel seriously ill. The truth is
I cannot distinguish the terrible weight from myself.
Overwhelmed with worry. My wife is growing.
She broke the news. She is pregnant

with our fourth.

Richmond Bridge

Richmond, Tasmania, is a quaint village well-established on the tourist map. Built upon a gruesome convict past it lays claim to Australia's oldest bridge. Built by convicts who quarried sandstone from nearby Butcher's Hill, this beautiful arched-bridge is said to be haunted by three ghosts.

Chief flogger and cruel overseer of the bridge's construction, George Grover, was ambushed by convicts one night, beaten to death and thrown into the Coal river below. Some claim he still wanders the riverbank and climbs the bridge's pylons.

The second ghost is a friendly black dog called 'Grover's dog'. It has been seen escorting school children across the bridge in the late afternoon before vanishing into thin air.

The third ghost is particularly strange. An old man with a walking stick, wearing a straw boater hat is said to appear upon the bridge. Others have seen him pushing a wheelbarrow and claim that he is sometimes 'headless'.

I booked into a haunted room at The Stables where blankets are ripped from the bed in the middle of the night and strange nose-bleeds are said to occur. From here I visited the bridge and surrounding sites at midnight, two am and four am.

Postcard from Richmond Bridge

In this light the ducks seem happily outnumbered,
coaches unload on the banks of the river. Tourists
stretch legs, releasing cameras and lunches, soaking up
the town's reflection. Beneath these arches tips of trees
are blazing like well-made kites. Reeds criss-cross
in murky nests promising tadpoles legs for tails.

A boy with a net, his pants cuffed high, stirs
the silt of the riverbed. With each careful step
bright scimitars clash, a crusade of light on stone.
Days have been tallied, like classes skipped, into
the bridge by convict picks. He swings his net,
inspects his catch, tourists charmed beyond belief.

But the coaches disappear as the fog sets in.
Ducks gather as a collection of pillows. Plumping
feathers they bury their bills, remembering the arc
of each toss. Until one protests, a disgruntled hoot
erupting upon the frost-bitten grass, dreaming perhaps
of his luck tomorrow paddling the autumn stills.

Portrait of a Headless Man Wearing a Straw Boater Hat

in straw boater hat and old fashioned clothes
he appears in daylight or after dusk
with a walking stick sometimes a wheelbarrow
wears a dark grey or pin-striped suit
always with a head but sometimes without
fits the description of a stranger or a local
he might have a limp but some say he doesn't
he is transparent or completely solid
and only on the bridge or along the riverbank
beneath the arches he climbs the pylons
wears a grey suit grey clothes some say pyjamas
he was drunk or fell asleep on the parapet
insulted a convict if not more than one
dashed by manacled hands or a spade
fell into the river some say he was pushed
his house was vandalised or else his grave
and always at night sometimes late afternoon
a large black or black and white dog
they are meant to be evil but this one's friendly
some call it Grover's it might not be his
escorts school children sometimes women
waits or vanishes before your eyes
an old bloke saw him walked or drove to the pub
downed three whiskeys but some say nine
then forgot his hat or his walking cane
perhaps a stranger most likely a local
collapsed on the road on the parapet of the bridge
they wheeled him home in a wheelbarrow

The Pitiless Grind

To save a convict's corpse from being dissected by the Surgeon General, it is
said his mates stole it and buried it quickly in the bridge's middle pylon.

look what we done you croppies
        look what you made of me
        stacked in the hulk of Butcher's Hill
you canary gang of thievers
        which one of you took the cat for this
        hauled me from the surgeon's slab
he would of dug me down to my quarry's fist
you done got me my ticket-of-leave
        feel the weight of them carts
        the ground pushes up
I am torn by what the present forgets
        what it claims to remember
        my ghostly council
there is a price to me beautiful grave

        me larcenous chums me iron gang
made me a plug in a funnel of stone
        these arches are shackles
        I am rationed by sand
mustered by the pitiless grind
        this river searching itself for salt
earth turning like a fiddle in the hand
        the sun's down-bow is playing me playing
I can almost feel the warmth
        you cursed me boys
you might have let me charge him
        the vinegar for rinsing me blood
still you done me the honour of what we all done best
        stealing without much of a plan

Introduced Species

Always these ghost stories of introduced species
a phantom dog, black cat, a spooky goat

Instead there should be tales of evil brush-turkeys
of posties swooped by ghoulish magpies

Sightings reflect the culture of the witness—
ghosts are no longer wearing chains

Mary only appears in Catholic countries—
it seems convicts are importing tales

At the edge of our roads possums and wombats
lie waiting to be recycled, pounds of colour

good for a yarn, each one on the nose

Still Night Jesters

nothing but the sound of my working jeans
      brushing through the fog
I am disappearing for a dying art
         swallowed by a tide of soup
where have all those pretty yarns gone
I will not see the graveyard until I'm in it
     a hunch
I am running   for the street-light's skirt
     running always makes it worse
         still   night jesters
    it quips   answers back
perhaps my days are not stalker-free
what I refuse to admit is behind that headstone
     I have brought my own ghost with me
pear-shaped and rotten
     pounding upon
         this feeble smear of light
the church tower chimes an extra hour
cock crows for the three hundredth time
     taunting me
that bloody bird on a pull-string for my denial
stepping out from the light
     concealing   coming clean
     confessional poet
         compulsive liar

Mindless Push

it is sheer dumb grit that leads me to
the point of no return each following step
requires even less thought a mindless push
to my power-stance as if posture can save me
from this big idea was a good idea at the time
I can move my body without parting the air
like a strict librarian resolute and resistant
watching myself far from the turning page
my mother's prayers the old benediction
as teeth chatter the sugar falls courage
is a trip-wire from cowardice one second
one extra breath to be held without thought
when common sense kicks in I exit like
a fuckin gunshot

Denial

the chill of the river is my rushed baptism
I knead the water as I knead the fog

I saw a figure on the bridge draped in white
hurl a package to a lonely splash

and then he stared down directly at me
I suggested a fencepost perched

the sound of escape each panicked step
shamed by this secret deliverance

the bag is sinking in final disgrace
I wade deeper toward the stash

sawn at the waist like a magician's assistant
wrists presenting the water's surface

hauling to the bank frost smeared with mud
my fingers ache upon this knot of denial

I have salvaged a weight a cold riddle
of meat the vessels in my hands

a placenta

Elvira
The Haunted
Hearse

Elvira is a 1967 Cadillac hearse originally owned by a funeral home in Pennsylvania. In her thirty-year career she carried approximately ten thousand people to their graves, clocking up 124,000 miles before being imported to Australia. This slick, black, twenty-one foot long vehicle is now the feature ride in a fleet of hearses that take people on ghost tours around Kings Cross and Sydney Harbour.

Passengers have reported nausea, headaches and strange pains while travelling in Elvira but it was not until 2005 that a ghost investigator braved staying overnight. This woman reported hearing laughter and voices from the driver's seat. She heard tapping upon the rooftop that moved around the perimeter in a pattern. On one occasion she claims she could see her feet surrounded by a strange blue light.

In 2007 I was the *second* person to stay the night.

Hit and Run

standing in front of the haunted hearse
      I feel a tingle in my legs
they say a force pushes out through the silver grill
is that a ghost or deep vein thrombosis
      it is hard to dismiss my imminent death
      drawn to dramatic irony
this year would make sense
      tonight of all nights
          the black polished page before me
the hood is reflecting my negative self
      number plate *RIP 100*
I will slot these pins into a sleeping bag
      the corners of a casual casket
wiggling my toes for reassurance
      it is time to signal this
          I have started to believe
beyond my own paranoia and the simple
      bodgy logic of others
which I have come to know well enough
      still some things don't add up
but it takes more than a tingle to support the fact
      waiting for the hit and run

Interpretation

trapped inside this morgue on wheels
spread flat as the things we hide in books
my warm breath coats the cold windows
wet planes for the scrawl of a ghost
locks stand ready to depress themselves
the door handles might refuse to budge
expecting a squall from the A/C ducts
the triggered yelps of a car alarm
my handycam creaks like an opening lid
I reach for the cheap shell of my torch
the odometer is ready to clock itself
radio tuned to the graveyard shift
latin on the dash *requiescat in pace*
might be a blessing tonight or a curse
pressed by the trial of interpretation
translates—may he rest in peace

3.33 am

three is an insult to the Trinity
three knocks from beneath the hood
three taps at the window, a blasphemy

the 'hottest' minute of the night
counting down, curling up, the ceiling
lined with pale stars, a white-sky

tribute to a roof I knew, one I gazed
up at for hours or a poster of Heaven
the interior light depicts a shape

at the centre of things, except now
it is cold, too much time to think
I am not listening hard enough

one for *yes*, two for *no*, if three is
profanity the classic six-six-six
must be out of fashion, does not fit

the clock so easily, tired of waiting
for the Devil's taunt or for God upon
the roof, three mates in one circle-dance

truth is I fell asleep

Unclean

I feel unclean in the morning
opening the door, releasing demons, my musty socks

the stench of the living
I role-played the dead, loaded myself in feet-first

closed my eyes
I drove myself to the front of the cavalcade

my favourite song
switched on the headlights, cruised in the left-hand lane

dawn rolled me out
I gripped the handle, tried to bear my waking self

hoisted my body
to shoulder height, tipped across the neat-snapped lawn

shaking the dream
I cannot shake what saved me from the ghostly touch

I turn around
something has printed WASH ME across my arse

EVP

The waveform charts an ambiguous sound
recorded at four am. A rise and fall amid the fuzz—
I admit there is interference. The engineer cuts
with the click of a mouse, isolating the event.
Confined to the studio, I am surrounded by terms,
Aux1, D-verb, 12 TalkBck. He tweaks the dials
with an arrow-hand, manipulates the trim, sails
a sea of 5.1 for a whisper in a storm. A siren
sings the briefest song, two syllables on repeat
rolling across my ear's taut drum. I am stranded
in this peculiar ship. Bent in devotion, closer
to the speakers, submitting my cheek for the slap.
The engineer says he is amplifying with 120db
of extra gain. I have been shanghaied again
behind polished glass, a space filled with shady
language. Just one clear word from the nebula,
some colour to this white noise. Stuck on a loop,
a listening trap, drawn late into the night. Death
works like this, stealing strips of life, feeding on
the prying mind. The engineer looks up, says
it is all *Greek* to him, charging extra for his time.
But the hint of one word is breaking me down.
My wife keeps txting me home.

Bunyips (3)

again my weight on the edge of your bed,
words fall like empty shells, your ticking clock is
Pinocchio's face, hands point to *always speak the truth*

my up-late brainteaser, I beg you to tell me
but your body is a ruthless mime, signalling all
that you refuse to say, scared words will turn to flesh

a shrug of your shoulders, you are locked,
it is late, I am so tired of this coming and going,
one day I will tell you of this grand adventure, what it did

and did not achieve, these long road-trips,
a night in a hearse cocooned in my sleeping bag,
I saw shadows spill over the ceiling's canvas, slide off

above my head, slowly at first, each one fell
the way I have become my poems, retreated to
my cluttered desk, I am disappointing to meet in person

stranded by language, designed for answers,
neat squares on a page of black, filling the boxes
with crude solutions, revising, we are grubby crosswords

down and across, the hands of your clock
trim away the night, as if time decides the rules
of the puzzle, keeps changing the frame around us

just lie down, we are safe for now,
it takes more than courage and words, waiting
to tell you of all I have seen, tonight I will not budge

Ultrasound

the monitor, a storm
of grey-weather tissue

radiographer steering
the echo's handle

clearing the squall
the eye of a profile

a heart, fine-
sketched, winking

stumps are crimped
buds emblems of

our fingers long ago
the image reset

story gestures, a wave
we cannot believe

we are part of this
remarkable smudge

teeth flaring, smile
of the spine

in my notebook a photo
of our native ghost

proof stuck between
all these words

Norfolk Island

Norfolk Island is situated in the South Pacific, approximately 900 nautical miles north east of Sydney. A remote convict settlement from 1788, it became known as the 'Ocean Hell', one of the most brutal penal colonies ever established. With rebellion a constant threat, beatings, floggings, torture and hangings without trial were common place. Decommissioned in 1855 the town of Kingston was resettled by Pitcairn descendants of Fletcher Christian and the famous mutineers of the Bounty.

Since their arrival there have been reports of strange lights in the Norfolk pines, of ghosts at the cemetery, Quality Row and in the ruins of the gaol itself. Some believe there are more ghosts per square kilometre than in any other region of Australia.

Perhaps the most haunted building is the Pier Store. Built by convicts, it is said to be home to a grey figure, a prisoner who drowned at Slaughter Bay. Oddly dressed, in a grey button-up suit and hat, he has been seen walking down the front stairs and out along the pier before disappearing into the ocean.

Once used as a storehouse, guardhouse, mill and coffin room, the Pier Store where I stayed is now a museum to the relics of the Bounty.

Of Angels and Demons

The radical preacher says ghosts are demons,
angels cast out of Heaven, known by their fruits—
Big Bang, Harry Potter and the theory of Evolution.
People need to be delivered from evil distractions.
He warns me against Norfolk Island. He saw a dvd
on the South Pacific. It is full of Mormon converts.
And poetry is a trap, one step from porn. He talks
about porn a lot. He asks me if I like American or
European. What exactly are we talking about?

If I attend his church he will release me from
my addiction to the occult. I admit I am haunted
by the spectre of prose, tempted in a desert of sales.
I have dabbled for fun with this other life, returned
to my difficult faith. Poetry fits, I hammer it out, often
devoid of love. He wants to drop me like a pine cone
from terrible height, crash me into outstretched limbs
falling at the speed of angels and demons. I wonder
how far he has spread his seed.

Kingston

The dwelling of demons in human shape,
the refuse of Botany Bay, the doubly damned.
                    — *Joseph Holt (prisoner)*

chain-gangs haul
across the reef quarrying
stone on the threat of the tide
one man falls, every man falls
cells are for murder at night
for boys to spread-eagle, high
on the wall, dark-red jets of blood
heads are struck like bells
strapped in the Bridle, the bit
of ironwood, chipping our teeth
meat we cannot cut, knives
hidden for revenge, imagine
the Commandant's belly open
raping his wife again, again
the gallows, drop fit for the noose
kingfishers perch on our graves
calm as executioners dressed
in black hoods, broken
we know how to rise

                    *

asleep you gaolers will hear us filing
we remain behind you in church in irons
at the cemetery's end, Hell on our shoulders
the ocean has washed us back up, damned
it could not flog us enough, we malinger
at your children's graves, scrawl a pentagram
above your beds, it is our turn now to watch
pleasing yourselves in pleasure gardens
escaping monkey puzzler trees, these pines
will be gallows for entire families, reflected
in Barracks' windows, building rebellion
like summer fog thick with expended life
tracing the wind, you wrought terror on us
we are Dumb Cell men without sound

Drowned Man's Bones

the wet-quarried store at the end of the pier
        a faint glow from the upstairs window
                small as a portal
        safe for now in my car
scouting the terror of a night in the ruins
beside me old whale boats are beached like cows
        that chew darkness on the edge of roads
        wide beasts in headlights
                fixed to the ground
the boats' stomachs are sprouting grass
        and soft-saw pines upon the cliffs
                teeth symmetrical to the moon
I will stare out from that window tomorrow night
        to the heart of the Pacific Ocean
        until a figure climbs out
comes walking toward me trapped in an old coffin room
        shitting myself
        I put my foot to the floor
        cattle grids are a drowned man's bones

The dead

after Kevin Brophy's *The dead* after Susan Mitchell's *The Dead*

The dead come down to the pier at night
their heads held high to the pines.
Igniting rough roads pot holes do not trip them
or the sound of country music in the distance.
They descend like the smell of boiled blubber on washing
asking questions so softly they cannot hear them.
They stare at paintings in the darkness of the gallery café
as close as they can get to dreams.
And glass cabinets in museums they want to open for us
to hold relics inside themselves, trying so hard.
We hear them only if they listen.
Some are plagued by the threat of informers.
Dressed in singlets, nighties or their Sunday best
a jumble of old theories and news.
Imagine them drifting down the hallway
to our sleeping faces, tying shells in the hair of our kids.

But at the end of the pier they wait upon
the ever-changing name of the moon and creatures before dawn
turning memory in the shallows
scraping bellies upon the rocks of the shoreline.

Pier Store (museum)

My weapons tonight include—
a cannon from the Bounty, old whaling spears
and the jawbone of a 47 foot Humpback.
I unroll my swag, attending it like a poem.
It is already neat but all I have. And relics
blasted from the ocean bed to a new museum floor.
An anchor of the Sirius weights a low moon,
a porch light for my ghost's arrival. At four am
the dying child on the breeze is a wild rooster
sick for dawn, hatching a banshee into the ruins—
the whale spears are attached to the wall.
I have waited now among so many stories,
all self-inflicted sores, rubbed powdered glass
and lime into my skin, watched the clock
tick down for hours. Enduring myself
at Slaughter Bay until morning lets me heal.
I walk out on the pier, looking back on an island
bristling with pin(e)s and needles.

Whaling Song

each tier of a pine tree is a curved whale boat
launched into the sea at dawn, lost at dusk
beacons are lit, soft language upon the horizon

a glowing ship marks the earth's turned side
steering on mutineers' blood, history is towed
like the Lord's Whale, boiled down, into song

enjambed, the living upon these stones broke
stones to anchor old dreams, from the work
of hands the shore is made, rowing forward

heaving back, rowing forward, *Come Ye Blessed*
memory like shadow is best stored upon itself
though darkness refuses to pass without trade

claim the red earth turned for good, climb
like a seed spread even on the wind, silhouette
upon the dawn, beneath the freshest star you are

here, departed, sing with us yourselves back home

Wielen Song

Translated by Archie Bigg

Dem lem orn a pain semes wan wiel boet
Se lornch et in em saf fas lait, en lors wen aa san sinken
Biik'n se lait et, sorf laengwij orn aa harais'n

Wan gloen shep se maak aa erth's tan saed
Stiaren orn em muuteniias' blad, se tua histri
Semes d' Lord's wiel, en se boil et daun iin wan song

Se jaam, dem wan lewen orn dii stuen bin brek a stuen
Fe einka dems uual driim, en from dems
Werken haan dem se miek shor, ruawen forad

Hiiwen baek, ruawen forad, *Come Ye Blessed*
Memri semes a shaedo baeta se stor et orn et saelf
Do daaknes nor musa gwena paas noe tried

Cliem em red dot se tan et fe guud, claim
Semes wan siid, se spred iiwen orn aa win, silhouette
Gen aa fas lait, anda da freshes staa haes yuu

Orl yorlyi, dem wan se gorn, cam sing yorlyi saelf
Baek hoem lorng fe aklan

Quarantine Station

I can only weep sadly to the moon
Separated from my parents by vast oceans
I have not reciprocated their love until this day

- Chinese engraving

The Quarantine Station is situated at Spring Cove on North Head, beside the popular suburb of Manly. In operation from 1828 to 1984 it is a small village with wharf, shower block, hospital, morgue and various buildings for accommodation. A total of 580 ships, 13,000 people, including immigrants and convicts were quarantined there for diseases such as smallpox, cholera, bubonic plague and Spanish influenza.

While the dead were quickly buried, many at night with no formal service, the healthy spent time swimming, playing quoits or engraving names and poems into the sandstone cliffs. Two thousand such engravings have been found.

Reports of three ghosts are common at the station—the matron, the Chinese man and the lost girl with pig-tail plaits. Virtually all of the buildings have some history of paranormal activity, the 'hottest' areas being the shower block, the hospital and the third class dining hall.

Dr Hawkins on the Lady McNaghten

the babies are dying the children infected we have only just begun
these free passengers torment each other unwilling to take my orders
I have emptied their luggage upon the deck we all must air our sheets
scrub with hot vinegar chloride of lime or none of us will disembark
someone is stealing the medicine I am bleeding to reduce the fever
meal and water all we have to eat powdered chalk to treat diarrhoea
parents consuming what is meant for their children and fighting
always fighting accidents births miscarriages typhus fever remains
chincough and measles cholera consumption mothers are dry of milk
lice have spread I will be blamed berths dark and filled with smoke
tipping the children into the sea what more can I do but bleed
mixing quinine to my cup of wine I need someone to lift my head
it is all my fault raise the yellow flag promise to obey me on this
no one can leave please tell them I am sorry when we are dead
they must burn the ship

Burials

wrap the body for me
I am not coming in
sew it up in a blanket
drag it over to the door
there is a coffin waiting
put it in and close the lid
but you have to hurry
I will bring fresh clothes
if it is done when I return
summon all your strength
the gravedigger is waiting
he is asking for his rum

towed to the station
the children are fevered
in this open whaleboat
the gravediggers argue
which coffins to carry
dying we hear their voices
stung with sea spray
at the top of the waves
all of us buried for drink
the curse of a widow
on these merciless thugs
sitting on the box
of my husband

I drive the horse
that hauls the coffins
quietly without delay
the moon's cold face
upon treated lids
disease scoffs at
the folly of names
no time for a blessing
the dirt is thrown
dirt will come at us
we are all infected
horse turning himself
back toward the wharf

Spring Cove

a village abandoned upon sandstone bluffs
the station pitched toward the wharf

anchored by history of occupation
a midden with harbour views, turned in

like the face of a cruel matron, fixed
to the boundary line, gripped

by a passage of fresh spring-water
trickling through the burial ground

the slow erosion of characters, names
engraved into the cliffs, worn

by the free patrol of rain
the speed with which stone forgets

buildings locked, each quiet verandah
wider than a haunted stage

a camp in cold witness, the reluctant
surveillance as time gradually awards release

This Arm That Never

This arm was cast from a smallpox victim,
manufactured in beeswax and ink, painted
yellow representing a jaundiced appearance
in a sealed glass box on felt. Note the size of
the pimples that filled with pus and erupted
upon clothes and linen, in the mouth at first,
across the palms, down to the soles of the feet.
See the wedding ring they could not take off.
We are invited to interpret the story. This arm
is fragile but in good condition, priceless as
a research tool. Check the painstaking length
the artist went to for our medical education,
donated to us by Sydney University, the victim
buried in an unmarked grave. Imagine it as
a ravaged gift, think how it must have played
a part, displayed here in our movable collection,
gambled on the voyage. This arm that never
stops retelling the story of its deadly cargo.
Reaching through time, swollen, resigned,
still untouchable.

Miasmas

the hurricane lamp in the Dying Room slowly swings itself
      before every death
          Matron Grieves in the doorway
          they are quietly wheeling you in
      the noxious fumes of your body decaying
polluted by an influx of stars
          planets in fatal alignment or
       emanations from the centre of the earth
              miasmas
      the sky is a toxic grave
the large onion at your feet absorbing
      coffins queue at the window as better skins
          waiting to seal you in
      this cruel lazaret
                beginning to rock
      Matron looms in the throws of light
          undoing her mask
          in stern defiance
          she sniffs the powdered scab

Morgue

everything finds the harbour
    even now
    from here
    laid out the cold body reducing

the smell of Phenol rushing the door
the brown bottles with necks for handles
designed to be tossed toward the sea packed with a scrawled SOS

just as we are designed
    to leak
    human
    juice collecting in the plug of the slab
drip by drip
the warp of our souls
seeping into the common drain

Fumigation

*Before release from the infirmary patients were ushered into a communal
steam room for the disinfection of air passages. Many were fully dressed and
had to walk in wet clothes up the hill to their new lodgings.*

fumigated like our mail
crammed into vapour baths
the chamber is shut, we open
our mouths, grateful to be alive
blessed by the violent spit and
hiss lining the forks of our lungs
we disinfect ourselves, moist air
collecting in deep-well scars of
faces, darkness drips, we are frail
cathedrals restored to catch the light
shadows woken, the hatch releases
we dutifully begin to climb, lugging
wet luggage past the burial ground
none stop to pay respect, aware of
the ghosts we might have become
steam pouring off our backs

Port Arthur

Established in 1830 as a remote penal settlement, Port Arthur was designed to break the spirits of the most hardened convicts. Deliberately overworked, underfed and inadequately clothed, prisoners did brutal hard labour in the timber yards, boat yard and coal mine. The slightest misconduct meant merciless flogging or incarceration in the Separate Prison where silence and isolation drove inmates mad.

Closed in 1877, Port Arthur is considered by many to be Australia's most haunted site. Its buildings and ruins come with established accounts of paranormal activity. But perhaps the most haunted is the vacant house where I spent the night, the Parsonage.

Dying in an upstairs room in 1870, Reverend Eastman's body was lowered out of the first-floor window whereby it fell to the ground and rolled into the gutter at the front of the house. Reverend Heyward and his family soon moved in and reported lights, floating figures, strange smells and knocking noises in the walls and floor. There have been similar reports up until the present day, including that of a builder who claims he was gripped around the throat by an unseen force.

Broadarrow Café

abruptly
your names the news

the present shook us
home

reminded then
of those we love

strangers we knew
were gone

        *

we looked to each other and television
until we fiercely turned it off, protective then,
helpless we imagined you standing, falling,
our living rooms broke open, the pain struck us
as parents or children in line, now the building
is a place we know inside ourselves, a garden
and a ruin, scored by loss we turn you over
defiantly working peace in

        *

trees are growing   the water is still
they say   these walls are touchstones

might we know ourselves here   a time
we believed   it could never happen here

a shell of a café   listening closely
for so many   better sounds

the brave who returned   a building
filled   with more than could be held

*

on the cross in the distance
we keep your names, a straight list
of what was stolen from us, every Sunday
we know that memories are prayers, still
they do and do not work, beside the water
we sit and think of you knowing that soon
we will have to leave, quietly hoping despite
so much grief—a father and all his tears

*

as if the pool is a wishing well, a boy approaches
with a coin his mother gave him, he stands at the words

of the reflective drum, *cherish, compassion, peace*
but as the coin begins sinking he tries to fish it out

his mother attempts to explain, wishes are sacred
because we let them go, keeping them within our reach

to see ourselves filled with bright things past
and in the dark spaces between, we are left to live

beside these words, cast again into the wind

Fabric (nightfall)

the cold crush of pebbled pathways
above my head bare-wire branches of oak
scraping winter, the twisted nick of claws
dark trunks are diaries of wood

upslope, hollow-mouthed, a cathedral
in shock, blessed only by wind and fire
stripped of ivy, a stone-tape plays back
murder, the energy of arches

my corner floor, inspecting the boards
a steep staircase and a locked piano
instruments left in this Imperial Prison
from nine o'clock this parsonage

a grim time capsule, past stored
inside the fabric of the present, reading
these rooms I will approach the dawn
and at dawn by reading be written

The Parsonage

There is a story from 1870 of a servant checking the guest room that she had recently washed out. Upon entering she saw the figure of a man in the window clutching a dagger, ready to strike.

smelling salt, cold water
a whiff of burnt feathers

the servant wakes, ears boxed
by the reverend, ringing

like the bell she answers
damp from wet floorboards

she points to the window, saw
a man with a knife, he lunged

at her until she fell, dropped
into the story of a haunted house

an account to outlast them all
picking her up, they close the door

keep quiet for the coming guest
fire crackling, chamber dries

like an edge of parchment crisped

Ghost Lines

midnight, I am staring at the nothing I have to stare at
dusk was a bright, tropical fish cooked in a bake oven arch
Gran is getting older, forgetting words, my kids are texting faster
in perfect line, my head, my body, a straight impersonation !
floating above me, caught in the flash, I prove my halo of dust
ripping the velcro on my laptop bag, afraid of what will wake
the good parson is dead, still upstairs, holding title to higher ground
between the ocean and forest in my sleeping bag, squirming out a poem
across the staircase, threads set for a ghost are snapping one by one
green button on a gate at the top of the hill—push to escape the grounds
on automatic, writing now, my cap as dirty as a hard-working mechanic's
in the light of my laptop, the ghost in the doorway mistaking me for a ghost

Bushfire

I dreamt a centipede gang of men
the felled-timber log on their shoulders

a dissection room spread with ash
sopping blood from the litter of limbs

convicts climbing paddle-wheel steps
the never-ending staircase turning

a corpse in the gutter of the parsonage
until the morning of the resurrection

the gravedigger-king on the Isle of the Dead
clearing his grave of worms

a powder monkey lighting the fuse
waiting to receive the blast

the convict-writer slitting his throat
to escape his life of debt

a festering spirit beside the baby's bed
spark of light as if striking a match

trapped in the chapel, a coffin-box pew
my boat for the coming flames

death at the end of a timber station
a bushfire that burns for days

Bunyips (4)

I am the thought, how the thought returns
the mind in cruciform, a panopticon structure
of routine, occupation, a prism for staring
breaking, morning comes with ticking hands
on watch ignoring the time, the dog-chain
at the gate, too busy to listen, linking
baby names to our own

*

I miss your school dress-up day—Hermione,
Captain Jack and Dorothy from the Wizard of Oz.
When I call in the morning you are posing for photos
on the steps in what your mother has sewn.

As if free from what haunts us, I will go to bed,
you will parade around the grounds with your class.
Ten long nights, I skirmished for words, then
what the birds and the dawn dispelled.

But every day, at different ages, new worlds
to understand, fears demanding to be arranged
among the frailty of fiction and names. Borrowing light
march ahead, though with each step you come apart

to meet the mystery within you, imagine this
there are mysteries you cannot imagine

*

now, at the end, metaphor, a chocolate trail of M&M's
the alien waddles, a bunyip roars for your new sister due in weeks

her ghost-black eyes, we will loom above her, giant shadows
she will come to trust, our familiar voices welcoming her

to such a terrifying, beautiful world

Going Home

...gotta testify, come up in the spot lookin extra fly
for the day I die, I'ma touch the sky...

On the phone to Australia at the side of the road,
today's filler for the talkback shows. Radio waves
in winter sun, wattle-blossom on every breath.

A carriage of words, leaving, returning, trucks
are hurtling past. I am rocked or still shaking,
receiving, transmitting what I do not understand.

Fielding their questions, eager to smoke the bees
in my chest to sleep. Tired of this awful drone.
Almost as painful as writing in public.

Hanging up now, back to Hobart, I will drive out
on that long causeway, wind tossing seals against
the side of the car, the saltwater I will crash through.

Shaped, a dub, filling the present. Tomorrow
I leave it behind. Now I am lighting up a cigarette
with a devilish grin, baring my belly to the sun.

Sources

AIPR Inc. 2002. 'Information Sheets' in Australian Institute of Parapsychological Research. accessed in 2006. from www.aiprinc.org

Bennet, Judith. 1999. *Quarantine Station, Manly*. accessed in 2007 from www.manlyquarantine.com

Flowers, B. Keuning, D. Stoermer, M. Vannucci, R. 2006. *When You Were Young: Sam's Town*. Universal-Polygram. NY. USA.

Foley, Jean Duncan. 1995. *In Quarantine: A History of Sydney's Quarantine Station 1828-1984*. Kangaroo Press. Kenthurst. NSW.

Gazzard, Albert S. 1983. *The Bounty and After*. Dorothy Mitchell. Palmerston North, NZ.

Goldie, Jan. (editor) 2001. 'The whole country's haunted: Australia's creepiest landmarks'. excerpts at The Haunted Bookshop. accessed 2007. www.haunted.com.au

Graeme-Evans, Alex. 1993. *A Short History Guide to Port Arthur 1830-1877*. Regal Publications. Launceston. TAS.

Hilton, Phillip and Hood, Susan. 1999. *Caught in the Act: Unusual offences of Port Arthur Convicts*. Port Arthur Historic Site Management Authority. Port Arthur, TAS.

Hitch, Gil and Maev. 1988. *Ghosts of Norfolk Island*. G & M Hitch. Norfolk Isl. South Pacific.

Hughes, Robert. 2006. on Enough Rope with Andrew Denton: Episode 129. 13/11/06. ABC. NSW.

Johnson, Diane and Kubrick, Stanley. 1980. *The Shining*. Warner Bros. CA. USA.

Jones, Granny. *Ghost Stories of Richmond, Tasmania*. Regal Publications. Launceston. TAS.

Jones, Granny. *Gossip and Facts about Richmond*. Regal Publications. Launceston. TAS.

Marrington, Pauline. 1981. *In the Sweet Bye and Bye: Reminiscences of a Norfolk Islander*. AH & AW Reed Pty Ltd. Sydney. NSW.

McCulloch, Julie and Simmons, Andrew (collators). 1992. *Ghosts of Port Arthur*. AD Simmons. Lauderdale, TAS.

Peters, Allan, L. 1992. No Monument of Stone: Elizabeth Woolcock's Struggle Through Life. Allan Peters. Christies Beach. SA.

Porter, Trevor J. 2000. *Gaol Ghosts: The Residents*. The Wednesday Press. Hamley Bridge, SA.

Porter, Trevor J and Towler, David J (collators). *The Hempen Collar: Executions in South Australia 1838-1964*. The Wednesday Press. Hamley Bridge. SA.

Pridmore, Walter B. 2005. *Isle of the Dead... Port Arthur's Burial Ground*. Walter B Pridmore. Murdunna. TAS.

Pridmore, Walter B. 2005. *Point Puer... and the Prisons of Port Arthur*. Walter B Pridmore. Murdunna. TAS.

Ryan, Reg and Olive. *Haunting Mysteries of Monte Cristo*. Junee, NSW.

Ryan, Reg and Olive. *Monte Cristo, Junee NSW*. Junee, NSW.

Smith, Nan. 1997. *Convict Kingston: A Guide*. Nan Smith. Norfolk Isl. South Pacific.

Storr, Will. 2006. *Will Storr vs The Supernatural*. Ebury Press. UK.

Thompson, Stephen. 2006. 'Objects through Time' in NSW Migrations Heritage Centre. accessed in 2007 from www.migrationheritage.nsw.gov.au

Vincent, Liz. 1997. *Ghosts of Picton Past*. Liz Vincent. Picton. NSW.

West, K. Smith, J. Jaco, W. and Mayfield, C. 2005. *Touch the Sky High: Late Registration*. Roc-a-Fella Records. NY. USA.

Yowie Man, Tim (the). 2006. *Haunted & Mysterious Australia: Bunyips, Yowies, Phantoms and Other Stranger Phenomena*. New Holland. Sydney, NSW.

Thanks to: Tim the Yowie Man, Todd Handy (Kurrajong Hotel), Jeff Fausch (Old Adelaide Gaol), Liz Vincent (Picton), Reg and Olive Ryan (Monte Cristo Homestead), Jim Cathcart (Fremantle Arts Centre), Alan Jennison (Richmond), Allan the Hearse Whisperer (Elvira the Haunted Hearse), Alison Lee (Quarantine Station), Brian Hubber, Maev Hitch and Archie Bigg (Norfolk Island), Jennifer Fitzpatrick and Andrew Ross (Port Arthur)

www.ingramcontent.com/pod-product-compliance
Lightning Source LLC
Chambersburg PA
CBHW030944090426
42737CB00007B/538